ARE YOU READY TO START YOUR OWN BUSINESS?

A Sanity Check for Those Who Dream of Self-Employment

CYNTHIA BAUGHAN WHEATON
The Entrepreneur's Friend®

Also by Cynthia Baughan Wheaton

**Extensive library of articles on
Our Work
and
Our Lives
at
www.TheEntrepreneursFriend.com**

For Jackson Baughan,
who showed me the
joy of business ownership.
Throughout my childhood,
my father was excited
to go to work
because he was the boss.
He was a quiet, steady man
of faith and family.

Thanks to him, I was ready.

For Jim Wheaton,
my editor and
my partner
in business, life and love.
Thank you for allowing me to
"drag you kicking and screaming"
into entrepreneurship.

Together, we were ready.

Contents

Chapter 1

The Reality of Self-Employment

"The best preparation for good work tomorrow is to do good work today."

Elbert Hubbard

≈

My father, an entrepreneur, would examine a problem and say to himself, "I can do that." Then, he did so – even if it required study, time or struggle. He would observe me facing a challenge and say, "You can do that." And I did.

My father's attitude – along with a viable business idea – is the basis of entrepreneurship. If we can imagine a business that is needed, and are willing to work as long and hard as necessary to make it happen, we can be self-employed.

The thought of business ownership can be both thrilling and terrifying, for good reasons. Thus, there is the need for a "sanity check," or honest evaluation. My mission is to help you with the decision-making process <u>before</u> you invest too much time, energy or money. There are important questions to answer and calculations to make before you proceed.

Specific questions are asked throughout this book, allowing you to identify the viability of your business concept. Answer them and you will be in a much better position to decide if entrepreneurship is for you.

Start with a Dream about the Future

If business ownership is your dream, you are not alone. Many people work for others, and look forward to the day when they can work for themselves. They want their compensation to be tied directly to the results of their efforts. They may be tired of working under someone else's rules, and want the freedom to set their own.

Some people become self-employed because there are no other viable options: they don't want to move, they were "right-sized" out of a job, they were not successful in their previous job, or their employer went out of business. Others are fortunate enough to develop or identify a needed product or service that can be sold at a profit.

You might want to start a medical or legal practice, a dairy farm, a retail store, or a construction business. You may be dreaming big dreams. Or, you may not even think of your work as a "business" – you are an artist, writer, musician, caregiver, or pet-sitter.

You belong to an exclusive group of brave and adventurous souls. What do you need to do in order to turn your dream into reality?

Building Blocks for Business Success

It is not hard to become an entrepreneur or small business owner.

It can be hard to become a <u>successful</u> entrepreneur.

Many have a skill or talent in demand, but do not know how to turn that into a thriving business. Thankfully, even in tough economic times, entrepreneurship can offer tremendous opportunity. Opportunity, however, does not mean success is easy, simple, quick – or guaranteed.

What are the building blocks of a viable business? They include:

- A product or service that is needed and/or wanted.

- A good price/quality ratio: a fair price for the quality offered.

- Accessibility: the target audience can buy it conveniently.

- Cost-effective marketing.

- The opportunity for profit after expenses are paid.

- Leadership from a passionate and dedicated advocate of the business.

- Sound management: common sense, knowledge, and experience.

- An engaged support team: vendors, employees, and others.

- Good cash flow.

- A well-considered business plan, incorporating all of the above.

Determine the Best Approach for You

You are unique in your abilities, dreams and desires. Start by identifying important questions and considerations. Your business may not include a single computer – ever. Or, you may want a highly sophisticated business that is technology-dependent.

Either way, you need to identify the essentials for success. Answer the questions that follow. Then, move forward if you believe you can make your business thrive and satisfy your personal needs.

Starting a Business is Like Beginning a Marriage

Every once in a while, we meet couples who were high school sweethearts. "We were too young and inexperienced to know what we were getting into," they say with a smile. Against all odds, they have gone on to have strong and healthy relationships for decades. We are wowed by their good fortune.

In the same way, some new businesses are started on a whim – without great forethought – and become wildly successful. However, the Small Business Administration reported in September 2012[1] that only one-half of new businesses survive five years, and roughly one-third of those started still exist after ten years.

In contrast, a recent study on first marriages by the National Center for Health Statistics[2] found 69% of couples made it to their tenth anniversary, and over 62% were able to celebrate their fifteenth. Thus, the average success rate for a new business is much lower than the likelihood of success for a first marriage.

My observation is marriages are more likely to succeed when the two individuals have discussed and agreed in advance upon their approach to the following key issues: 1) money, 2) children, 3) religion, 4) intimacy, and 5) any other

---

[1] SBA Office of Advocacy, Frequently Asked Questions about Small Business, September 2012; page 3. https://www.sba.gov/sites/default/files/FAQ_Sept_2012.pdf

[2] Monthly Labor Review, October 2013, Table 6. Bureau of Labor Statistics, United States Department of Labor, http://www.bls.gov/opub/mlr/2013/article/marriage-and-divorce-patterns-by-gender-race-and-educational-attainment.htm

factors critical to one or both of them, such as geographic location.

Love by itself is not enough to make a marriage last. Love must be combined with strength in order to withstand the ups and downs of marriage and life. Mutual commitment provides that strength. With over twenty-eight years of successful marriage behind me, I know this to be true.

Like marriages, new businesses are more likely to succeed when they are built upon a foundation of commitment and communication. Be honest with yourself – and others – as you explore a potential commitment to business creation.

Self-Employment Impacts Work and Life

When we work for someone else – particularly in certain fields – work is work and home is home. Week nights and weekends are focused on personal activities. When we are self-employed, and want to be successful, these lines blur. Especially when our business is first getting started, is in a slump, or is growing rapidly, we have to make personal sacrifices.

The good news is the work/home lines blur in the other direction as well. It can be easier to arrange time out of the office. We can incorporate our passions into our work in creative ways. We can become highly productive and more balanced over time if we – and our household – accept the new normal.

As the owners of a consulting business, my husband and I have found a number of personal benefits:

- Non-work priorities (e.g., children, parents, hobbies, service work, and health care appointments) fit more easily into our schedules. A personal week-day event may mean working nights or weekends, but the choice is ours.

- We stopped fearing the inevitable job changes and corresponding geographic relocations. We did not want to move any more – especially when we had children at home.

- When we are sick, we can take a nap every few hours. Then, go back to work as necessary.

- We can go to the gym, or to the supermarket, when it is not crowded.

- If there is a family crisis or a fun opportunity, we can take our computers and travel as needed. When our daughter suffered a serious concussion while attending college in a distant city, I was able to work from her apartment.

- Our kids have learned a significant amount about business, economics and other issues related to what we do. As a result, we have more ways to relate as a family.

- Our commute is short. We work at home, saving time and money.

- Working together as a couple has strengthened our relationship.

- Our children always know where to find us, and we are able to touch base with them whenever one of them wants or needs to do so.

- We can be with our pets. Our cats keep me company most days. Walking the dog is a great mental and physical break from my computer screen.

On the other hand, we have made personal sacrifices:

- Sometimes we have had to miss important family events because of travel or other work commitments.

It can be even harder to explain these priorities to those you love when it is your decision – and not the decision of your boss.

- We have had to consciously choose not to let work conversation dominate the family dinner.

- During the first ten years of our business, when our children were young, most family vacations were at the beach. We would rent a house, and take much of our equipment: computers, printer, and even a fax machine. We labored inside during the hot afternoons, and returned to the beach later in the day. More times than we can count, a crisis arose that needed to be handled immediately.

For my family, business ownership has added to the quality of our lives – in many ways. My hope is you will benefit from my experiences and observations in order to create a successful business for yourself.

There Are No Guarantees

Most new businesses do not succeed. That is a fact and we all need to accept it. At the same time, we can minimize the chance of failure.

Besides, what are the alternatives? Typically, there are no guarantees of success, or even continued employment, when we work for others.

Important Disclaimers

No book can address all of the specifics of each reader's life, business idea and financial situation. The content of this book is pulled from my life-long connection to entrepreneurship – my experience, musings and observations. By its nature, reading a book is different from having a consulting relationship built on extensive two-way communication.

You must determine how detailed you need to be in examining and building on the possibilities presented here. Obviously, a part-time maker of pottery will have fewer issues to address than someone starting a small manufacturing firm.

The goal of the book is to provide a number of deciding factors to help you identify and think through key issues, put together a solid plan, and set reasonable expectations. The questions in each section will help you determine your readiness to proceed.

Working through the issues and questions posed in the pages ahead will not guarantee success. However, with honest examination, each positive response will increase the likelihood of success. Likewise, too many negative responses should result in a decision to re-think, re-group or walk away.

Chapter 2

Deciding Factors:
Open Eyes, Open Mind, Open Heart

"In order that people may be happy in their work,
these three things are needed:
They must be fit for it.
They must not do too much of it.
And they must have a sense of success in it."

John Ruskin

~ ~

Know Yourself

Self-employment is a process and a lifestyle. As such, it needs to start with you, the "self." An honest self-examination can help smooth the path to success. Whether working in our small businesses, or leading our non-business lives, we can become happier and more confident if we have a realistic sense of our selves.

It troubles me to hear people say, "You can be whatever you want to be." That is not true. If we do not have good visual skills, we can improve them with training but we are unlikely to be successful designers or decorators. When intellectual gifts are average, we probably will not qualify for graduate school in bio-engineering. If we do not have good eye-hand coordination, we can improve but we will not develop into Olympic champions.

Personal requirements for successful business ownership

There are many personality traits, skills and abilities that contribute to the development of a profitable business. However, these seven personal ingredients are required for entrepreneurial success:

- Determination to reach goals.
- Passion for the industry, product or process.
- Sufficient physical and mental energy.
- Courage to make and act on decisions.
- Strong work ethic.
- Smart enough.
- Credibility.

How many of these seven requirements do you meet?
All   Most   Some   None

Are you willing to develop, or compensate for, the ones you are currently missing?
Yes   Maybe   No

Personal Readiness Inventory

With the understanding that we all have limitations, success is still possible. In addition to the seven requirements just listed, what are your relevant assets and deficiencies? Your likelihood of success will increase for each asset you possess.

Personality

- Are you a <u>practical thinker, with common sense?</u> For many small business owners, intelligence is not as important as common sense.

- Are you a "<u>people person</u>"? A willingness to engage with others helps establish new relationships quickly.

- Do you <u>reflect</u> on the world around you? More introverted people tend to be particularly good at issues that benefit from thoughtful consideration.

- Are you <u>willing to be in charge?</u> You do not have to be a control freak to be successful – in fact, tight control can be counter-productive. You do need to be willing to take responsibility in every way.

- Are you <u>willing to be direct</u> with others? When you own a business, the need to say and do difficult things occurs regularly.

- Can you <u>control your temper</u>? Frustrations and negative surprises will be plentiful and anger is rarely helpful in achieving business goals.

- Are you <u>flexible</u>? The only constant in today's business world is change. Any entity needs to evolve in order to survive. Even external factors such as technology can change at a breathtaking rate, disrupting your business if you do not adapt.

- Do you have <u>intellectual curiosity</u>? Success is more likely when you actively explore issues relevant to your business.

- Do you know how to <u>manage your mood</u> in difficult situations? Sitting alone and trying to figure out how to start a business can be daunting. Isolation can be particularly difficult for anyone who is prone to depressive moods or who has recently been through a major loss. If depression occurs, it is critical to recognize that and get external support. Professional help, available in most communities, can accelerate the healing process and help you focus on life goals.

Skills and Abilities

- <u>Comfortable with numbers</u>? Excellent. Numbers are necessary for financial planning and evaluating business results. If math is an area of weakness, take a community college course, or partner with someone you trust who has solid quantitative skills.

- <u>Pick up new ideas quickly</u>? Some people explore new possibilities easily – which helps build faster momentum for growth. Others need more time and should plan accordingly.

- <u>Creative thinker</u>? Businesses thrive when new solutions are found for old problems. However, even if you are not particularly creative, you can benefit from adding the input of others to your own informed observations about your marketplace.

- Are you able to <u>juggle multiple priorities</u>? Running a business requires you to keep an eye on income, costs, employees, customers and more. If you are energized by managing several projects at once, that is a good indication of potential success.

- Do you <u>manage money responsibly</u>? If you own a business, your financial future will be controlled by you.

Some people are so cautious it is difficult for them to invest in a business. However, thoughtful spending is an essential ingredient for success.

- Able to <u>focus for long periods</u>? Some business challenges require steady – and sometimes even intensive – focus. If you are blessed with the gift of extended focus, pursue competitive advantages that benefit from it. At the same time, do not get so absorbed you have trouble completing necessary tasks.

- Are you a <u>good judge of character</u>? Determining whom to trust and whom to avoid is essential. "Trust but verify" is an excellent motto.

- Can you be <u>tactful when you are trying to be persuasive</u>? If you are thoughtful and considerate, you generally will be more effective.

- Do you <u>like to plan</u>? Thinking through next steps in a logical order comes more easily to some than others. Without planning, more problems – even catastrophes – will result.

- Are you <u>process driven</u>? Do you like to find ways to increase efficiency and/or effectiveness?

- Can you be <u>productive when working alone</u>? If you are used to working in a large organization, the loneliness of a start-up can be a shock.

- Can you <u>make good decisions quickly</u>? Often there is not time to thoroughly analyze a situation before making a decision. If needed, enlist an experienced and trustworthy person to help, even if compensation for their services is necessary.

- Do you have <u>keyboard proficiency</u> (i.e., know how to type)? Work will be much easier if you do not have to rely on others to produce professional-looking documents.

- Can you <u>inspire others</u> to work together on a common goal? Getting everyone on the same page is a critical element of leadership.

- Are you a <u>good listener</u>? Opening your mind to the ideas and concerns of others can help grow your business while minimizing challenges.

Experience

- Have you ever <u>observed an entrepreneur close-up</u> (e.g., parent, family friend, sibling or best friend)? Witnessing the struggles and satisfactions of self-employment can provide helpful perspective.

- Have you ever <u>managed people</u> in a work environment? Good management skills are essential to retaining employees and accomplishing business goals.

- Have you ever <u>hired or fired</u> someone? If so, you will be able to better perform both in the future. If you can hire well, you may be able to entirely avoid the firing process.

- Do you know how to organize, supply and <u>run an office</u>?

- Do you have the <u>computer proficiency</u> required for internet searches, ordering supplies, tracking expenses, handling the inevitable IT problems, and more?

- Do you have <u>good self-knowledge</u>? Do you understand your strengths and weaknesses? Whatever you know about yourself today, you will learn more through this process.

- Have you ever <u>experienced failure</u> or deep disappointment? If so, you will likely do a better job of avoiding or dealing with it in the future.

- Do you know how to <u>conduct focused and productive meetings</u>?

- Are you a <u>good negotiator</u>? Do you understand what it takes to arrive at a fair agreement?

Character

- Are you <u>humble</u> enough to take care of any necessary task? Start-ups rarely have administrative assistants or employees. You need to do just about everything yourself. Are you willing?

- Are you <u>persistent</u>? There will be plenty of obstacles for which you need to find solutions. If you make the commitment to start a business, you need to be able to keep moving forward.

- Are you <u>dependable</u>? Your reputation will be built on your ability to keep promises made to employees, clients and vendors. If you say you will do the work at a certain time, or for a given price, you need to do so. When promises cannot be kept, changes need to be communicated on a timely basis.

- Are you willing and able to <u>say "No!" to yourself</u>? You will not have a boss to stop you if there are signs of trouble.

- Are you <u>patient</u>? Business goals are rarely met as quickly as we hope or plan. That does not mean they cannot be reached. In addition, patience with others can minimize turbulence in your work and in your personal life.

• Are you <u>honest with yourself</u>? It can be easy to fool ourselves if we are committed to a particular outcome. If your business plan indicates the need for significant alterations, can you face the truth and deal with it appropriately?

• Are you <u>committed to the continued support of those you love</u>? Financial support is not enough. Your loved ones will also need you to recognize and meet their non-financial needs. Ignoring the needs of those closest to you because of start-up commitments can take a heavy – and even unacceptable – toll.

• Are you willing to extend your energies into the "non-dollars-and-cents" areas of the business, in order to <u>aid co-workers and employees in caring ways</u>? Emergencies will happen. A business owner who makes hospital visits, prays for and with employees, and offers generous benefits to those who are in crisis, will have a loyal staff and potential new hires who are clamoring to come onboard.

Mindset

• Can you <u>create your own structure</u>? Businesses do not thrive in chaos and neither do most people. One of the most challenging aspects of a new venture is the lack of an initial framework. One of the first priorities is to create your own structure – and then build on it by enforcing self-imposed deadlines.

• Are you <u>willing to delegate</u>? From the beginning, before you are in a position to hire your first employee, you may need to delegate to sub-contractors. As the business grows, you cannot keep doing everything you did at the beginning. You must be willing to let go of selected responsibilities, assign them to others, and verify as needed. Hiring good people, and trusting them to do their jobs, is essential for the growth of your business.

- Have a <u>thick skin</u>? In these days of social media, an anonymous public can give mean-spirited, even un-warranted, criticism. Owners who are overly sensitive can be blindsided by such drama, taking needed focus away from business operations. The best solution? Learn whether to ignore or address such situations.

- Willing to <u>go outside of your comfort zone</u>? Self-em-ployment stretches you to do tasks you may have relied on someone else to do. A woman I know was commit-ted to establishing a house cleaning service. Her big-gest problem? She was uncomfortable returning calls from potential clients. The solution? Set a deadline to do what you dislike in a timely fashion – and then force yourself to do it.

- Can you <u>deal with fear</u> of the unknown? The future is always in the back of a business owner's mind. Every-one fears it to some degree. Use your fear as motiva-tion to plan well and work hard. Have faith you will find a way, on your own or with assistance, to conquer whatever difficulties arise.

- Do you have <u>sufficient motivation</u> to keep working hard? A hobby is something done in your spare time. A business requires ongoing dedication. Many small businesses – especially home-based entities – gener-ate a minimal income because they are a hobby, or experiment, and the owners do not put in the time or effort required to be successful.

- Can you set work aside and relax, even when there is a never-ending list of tasks to complete? Burnout is a too-common problem for business owners. You will need to spend reasonable amounts of time doing what you love with the people you care about. Otherwise, you will set yourself up for failure.

- Are you willing to be responsible for providing significant household income for some, perhaps many, of your employees? Their lives will be directly linked to your success.

- To whom will you be accountable? Is that sufficient to keep you on track?

- Are you a big picture person? Can you envision where the business needs to go, and the most important ways to get there?

- Are others included in your definition of success? Working for more than our selves can increase motivation.

- Are you a confident person? If you do not believe in what you are doing, neither will anyone else.

- Are you fired up by considering this list? If not, you have just learned an important – and relatively inexpensive – lesson.

Which of these attributes do you have? How will you use and develop them within your new business? How can you compensate for your weaknesses so they will not hold back the development of your business?

Again, you do not have to be perfect. However, the more of these traits you have – or develop – the better your chances for success as a business owner.

Do you know yourself?
Yes   Somewhat   No

Out of the fifty-four attributes in the Personal Readiness Inventory, how many describe you?

In which areas are you strong?
Personality   Skills & Abilities   Experience   Character   Mindset

Are you willing to get training, bring in a partner, or hire someone who has the necessary traits you are missing?
Yes   No

Know Your Product or Service

Whether you are considering a business built around an existing expertise of yours or something entirely new, you need to have intimate knowledge of your product or service. Are there needed improvements no one else has made? What are the opportunities?

It is important to understand the underlying financials. You will need these in order to put together a Financial Plan, as described in Chapter 4. For example:

- What will be the average selling price?

- How much will it cost to produce? Will the cost change if the quantity increases?

- How much up-front capital investment is required to buy machinery, outfit an office or establish a retail outlet?

- How many skus (i.e., stock keeping units, or individual inventory items) will you need to maintain?

- Even if your business is as simple as selling your consulting services by the hour while working out of your home, what will it cost to market your business and bring on new clients or customers?

<u>Become an expert on the specifics</u> necessary to make it and sell it. One route is to work for someone else in order to learn the business. A friend who wanted to start her own child care center determined her first step should be to work as an employee at an existing daycare. For now, she is learning everything she can while receiving a steady paycheck. Her goal of self-employment becomes a more viable option with every passing day.

Another path is to <u>establish yourself as an expert in your field</u> while still employed elsewhere. My husband did extensive speaking and writing in our industry while working for others, establishing his credentials as a knowledgeable source. His proven expertise, including a large body of published articles, became the early foundation for our consulting firm.

Over time, the process of establishing expertise becomes self-perpetuating. If you do thorough research on a topic in order to produce a quality article or speech, you are building your business knowledge. If you are going to give a speech and have to prepare for questions, you expand the expertise you can offer to customers. Writing a proposal and getting feedback – even if it is negative – can help you in the future.

Do you know your product or service?
Yes   Somewhat   No

Understand Geographic and Lifestyle Considerations

A forward-thinking member of the United States military decided to invest in a small business, preparing for an eventual return to civilian life. He purchased automatic ice-making equipment and wisely located it next to a high-traffic intersection. The product is 1) frequently needed, 2) priced well, and 3) easily accessible. Unfortunately, there were several issues he overlooked – or underestimated:

- The equipment is located in his home town, where he plans to live in the future. Currently, he lives hundreds of miles away. His retired father replenishes bagging supplies regularly, refusing any payment. What happens if his father becomes incapacitated?

- The owner's cell phone number is posted for customer service. He gets calls 24/7/365. Some are legitimate, but most are from people who 1) did not read the clearly posted instructions, or 2) are placing crank calls. A difficult situation will be even more challenging during his next overseas deployment.

If you do not live nearby, can you afford to pay someone to take care of the day-to-day needs? You should not count on family or friends to provide services for free.

If your business idea requires weekend or evening work (e.g., restaurants and retail stores), have you accounted for the impact on social and family needs or obligations? It is one thing to choose to work on weekends, but some businesses require it – every week. Now is the time to honestly consider geographic and lifestyle issues – before you invest.

Can you afford to pay every worker a reasonable wage on Day 1?
Yes   No   Maybe

Will your efforts be concentrated within a manageable geographic area?
Yes   No   Somewhat

Will you be required to serve customers on weekends and/or holidays?
Yes   No   Maybe

If so, will this be acceptable to you long term?
Yes   No   Maybe

Know Your Target Market

One of the most important lessons for prospective start-ups is few businesses can grow and survive by selling exclusively to friends and family. The most supportive in your personal circle may not need or want your product, even if it is appropriate for them. If someone you know does make a purchase, he or she might not buy again. This can be disappointing, but is often the case. You must prepare to sell to a wider market of prospective buyers.

The target market (i.e., target audience) consists of the potential buyers of your product or service, and especially the ones with the most interest. If you can identify your target audience, you can focus your energy, time and financial resources in a more productive way.

Overall, these are the people who need or want what you are offering. Sit back and visualize your ideal customers. Who are they?

Will you be selling to individual consumers or to other businesses? Although many businesses sell to both, most focus on one or the other – at least to start.

Can your target consumers be identified by their demographics? These factors are used to define individual consumers. Data relevant to your specific business is the most helpful, and might include:

- Geography/location.

- Gender.

- Age.

- Income.

- Credit worthiness.

- Education.

- Presence of children.

- Age of children.

Can your target consumers be identified by their psychographics (i.e., lifestyle characteristics)? These specific needs or interests can help identify and target your best prospects. For example, if your best customers are video gamers, you have insight on where to search for them, and how the advertising should look. Other examples of psychographics include:

- Avid reader.

- Antiques lover.

- Animal advocate.

- Organic farmer.

- Coffee drinker.

- Classic car buff.

- Frequent live-concert attender.

Can your target business audience be defined by firmographics? These are the equivalent factors for companies selling directly to other businesses instead of consumers (also known as Business-To-Business or B2B marketers); for example:

- Geography/location.

- SIC code. The Standard Industrial Classification is maintained by the United States Department of Labor.

- Number of employees.

- Annual sales.

For some of you, there is an additional layer or middle-man between you and the end-user of your product or service. If you are a writer, the first hurdle may be to target an agent or publisher. Of course, one of the skills any middle-man will be looking for is whether or not you understand your target audience.

Generally, the more specific the target market, the smaller the number of people who will qualify as targets, and the more interested they will be in what you have to offer. For example, many years ago a company was researching possible new book titles. There was one subject only a small percentage of book buyers cared about, but their interest level was extremely high. The subject was the Vietnam War. The company doing the research decided not to pursue the topic because too few people in small focus groups were interested, and some were decidedly negative. However, a competitor came out with a series on the same topic a year later. It was highly successful.

Once you can picture your target audience, begin to focus your marketing efforts in a cost-effective way. For instance, list brokers can provide mailable names and addresses based on many of the criteria listed above. Or, you can attract potential customers via targeted social media accounts. Perhaps local cable channels offer cost-effective contact during programs your target market is likely to watch.

Use caution and move slowly with higher-cost media, or those requiring a substantial time commitment. They can create a big hole in your budget or your time, and still disappoint.

In the end, your target audience needs to be "just right" in size: specific enough to understand, but large enough to generate sufficient revenue.

Have you identified your Target Market?
Yes   Somewhat   Not Yet

Know Your Industry, Including the Competition

Businesses reflect the industries they serve. Decades ago, a family friend had steady income with a television repair business. In their early days, televisions had vacuum tubes known for blowing out periodically, much like light bulbs. They required specialized repair. Demand for his services declined rapidly as technology advanced, forcing him into early retirement.

Another friend became the third generation to run the family manufacturing business. As competition shut down or moved overseas, he developed a new approach to keep the business local and retain loyal employees. He developed a niche product built with the company's existing equipment and processes, but added a novel twist to make it cost-_inef_fective to import. Years down this new path, the business is thriving.

Before any business is started, it is critical to understand the competition and the industry. Key questions include:

- Has there been growth, stagnation, or steady decline in the past five or ten years?

- How have technological innovations changed the industry? Are there new technologies on the visible horizon?

- Are there high barriers to entry, such as extensive capital investment or rare expertise? Or, can anyone with a computer and a phone build a business?

- Is there an opportunity for a new approach, otherwise known as a unique selling proposition, or USP? A USP can be defined by a patented technique, higher service level, advantageous pricing model, higher-quality standard, or some other key variable to differentiate you from your competition.

Become informed about your industry.

- Subscribe to trade publications, blogs and websites, immersing yourself in the key issues of your chosen market niche.

- Attend industry conferences and seminars, if available.

- Develop and nurture professional relationships.

- Follow industry leaders on social media.

- Keep reading until the subject matter begins to repeat, and then scan for updates on an ongoing basis.

Legal requirements are essential to understand before launching a business, and may vary by region or community. No one wants to invest time, money and effort in a business with no legal right to exist.

- Pay particular attention to zoning laws.

- Be sure there is there are no infringements on existing patents, copyrights or trademarks.

- Determine if there are any other legal constraints.

The excitement we have for our wonderful ideas can dissipate quickly if we discover someone else already offers the same product or service. However, we may still be able to do it faster, with better service, or cheaper. Starting with the basic concept of an existing product or service, and improving it in some way, is a good thing – as long as you do it legally.

Does success in the industry depend on political connections? If so, beware. For example, the owner of a security firm once confessed a hefty donation to the local sheriff's election was required to ensure prompt responses when an alarm went off at any of his client's locations.

Political connections may appear to offer a quick start for a new business, but political winds can be fickle. Use caution, or political demands for time and money can consume the resources required for you to build and strengthen your business.

In addition, environmental issues need to be fully understood. Beyond related legal ramifications, there may be opportunities available to those who can offer "green" alternatives.

In the 1960's, a friend's father was working in a highly-toxic industry. His success in inventing an environmentally-friendly replacement process was not only ahead of the environmental movement, but was the foundation for a family business with decades-long success.

Do you have a solid understanding of your industry?
Yes   Somewhat   Not Yet

Are there significant barriers to entry?
Yes   Maybe   No

Are you willing and able to deal any with any political pressures?
Yes   Maybe   No

Are there specific legal concerns tied to the industry?
Yes   Maybe   No

Are there environmental concerns?
Yes   Maybe   No

If there are concerns, do you have a plan to overcome them?
Yes   Maybe   No

Know Your Personal Financial Situation

Having a conservative approach to financing a business has always served me well. When I started new ventures within corporations, everyone agreed on the level of required investment prior to the actual outlay of much, if any, money. Self-employment should proceed in the same way.

When my father, Jack, was a young man, he and his identical twin moved from their rural home to the "big city" to make their fortune. They were a team. Lee drove a city bus, supporting them both while my father attended trade school. Jack studied carpentry, drafting, plumbing, masonry, and more. Once his training was complete, Jack started a business, growing it until it could support the two brothers. Then, Lee joined him.

Ideally, a small business start-up needs a solid financial base. The amount of financing required will vary depending on your particular situation. In general, clear economic advantages exist if you have two or more of the following:

- A dual-income household in which one person will keep his or her day job – and, ideally, health insurance – while the other acquires training or works, without pay, on the new business for some period of time.

- Savings, not to be invested in the business, equal to at least six to twelve months of living expenses.

- No monthly debt other than a reasonable mortgage.

- No large personal expenditures required in the immediate future, such as for a baby, college tuition, an extravagant wedding, major home renovations or a new house.

- A Plan B that can be quickly implemented if the new business does not succeed.

If you do not know your <u>personal credit score</u>, this is a good time to get it. The score is a measure of credit-worthiness based on a number of factors, including existing debt and timely bill payment. Once you know your score, you will have a better sense of your ability to borrow money.

Most importantly, <u>if you have a spouse</u>, include him or her in all of the big financial decisions. Any new business involves time, money and energy – and will directly impact your relationship. Thus, your spouse is your business partner. Be sure you work together to define personal investments and any credit risk to be taken, such as a second mortgage or loan.

I have heard of people who are not forthcoming with their spouse about the family's financial situation. If this is your practice, your spouse would be in a financial quandary if you were to become physically or mentally impaired – or worse. Such lack of communication does not reflect the type of open and honest relationship I have found to be fruitful and rewarding. If married, talk honestly about the best way forward for you and your spouse.

Do not invest more money in your new business than you can afford to lose. Once your investment is made, it becomes a sunk cost – one paid in the past and, in many cases, gone forever. Thus, you need to approach your start-up as a prudent risk, and not a reckless gamble. The good news is, if you do your homework well, you will have a much better chance at winning than you would ever have at the slot machines.

How many of the five financial advantages (listed above) do you have?
5   4   3   2   1   None

If you have a spouse, is that person a willing financial partner?
Yes   Somewhat   No

Do you have someone to help you by "driving the bus"?
Yes   No

Examine Your Non-Financial Obligations

Time has a way of disappearing as a new business grows. What are your family obligations? What about any service commitments in your community?

When my husband and I started our business, we had two young children. I limited their extra-curricular activities, giving them the time for unstructured creativity at home where we were available. Thus, we minimized the stress of family logistics, and our children learned to entertain themselves.

In addition, I resigned a demanding volunteer leadership position, eliminated participation in ongoing committee meetings, and opted for service projects I could do on my own schedule. As our work schedule became more predictable over time, I took on service projects to fit my availability.

Re-consider your "optional" commitments at work and at home. Unless you are passionate about them, drop them – at least for a while.

Have you dropped or pared back non-essential obligations?
Yes   Somewhat   No

If not, are you willing to do so?
Yes   No

Identify Your Support Team

Every business owner needs a support team, even if it is an informal one. When times are mentally, physically or emotionally demanding, it is helpful to know we have people who will encourage and comfort us.

The most likely sources are:

- Family.

- Friends.

- Self-employed peers, even if in a different industry.

- Local faith community.

Do not underestimate the value of sharing concerns honestly with others who are in a position to listen, inspire or motivate, while respecting confidentiality.

Do you have people who will actively support you?
Yes   No

If You are a Person of Faith

"Yahweh is near to all those who call on him,
to all who call on him in truth."

Psalm 145:18 (World English Bible)

Deciding to start a business is likely to be one of the biggest decisions of your life. If you are a person of faith, you will want the process to be the subject of prayer.

Give thanks for every opportunity, regardless of the eventual outcome. Express gratitude for God's presence as you evaluate your options – whether you are happy, overwhelmed or in turmoil.

Asking God for much-needed discernment can be both helpful and reassuring. Confess any personal insecurities, poor decisions or harmful mistakes. Ask for help dealing with your personal deficiencies honestly and productively.

Pray for the people who will become your employees, partners, clients/customers, vendors and personal support team. Express thanks for the encouragement, patience and understanding of those who surround you.

Also, ask for energy, focus, and clear priorities. They are essential to success.

Open yourself to God's guidance and inspiration. He may lead you to opportunities and people you may not have otherwise identified.

Are you tapping into the power of prayer?
Yes   No

Chapter 3

Deciding Factors: Input from Others

"Where there is no counsel, plans fail;
But in a multitude of counselors they are established."

Proverbs 15:22 (WEB)

~ ~ ~

Almost everyone is willing to give an opinion about our work and our lives, often without being asked. Sometimes opinions are helpful, but not always appreciated. Sometimes others lead us astray, even when they have the best intentions.

When looking at self-employment, we need to weight more heavily the insight from people who know us well – and whom we trust. If you have a trusted family member or friend who believes it would be a big mistake to start a business, do not ignore their concerns. Instead, methodically investigate your options, even if – ultimately – you convince only yourself.

For example, I have a good friend who thought it would be a terrible idea for Jim and me to start our consulting business. However, her concern was based on her husband's experience of starting a business, only to end up facing financial ruin.

As we reflected upon our own planned startup, we realized the circumstances were entirely different from those of my friend's husband, and the corresponding amount of financial risk we were taking was comparatively modest.

Have you gotten input from people you trust?
Yes   No

Business Owners

As with many aspects of life, it is difficult to visualize something unless you have already done it yourself. Therefore, other small business owners can be great resources, even if they are not in your industry. Sharing your idea of self-employment with family and friends may lead you to valuable contacts.

Trade groups can be helpful, as can local business groups. The Chamber of Commerce is a tremendous resource in many communities, offering a variety of business connections in your area. In addition, seek out local Business Incubator services which are increasingly provided by colleges and communities. Also, social media offer connections to business owners in similar circumstances, some of whom can be remarkably helpful.

Mutual respect is an important sign of professionalism. When you communicate with other business owners, respect the possibility they may have trade secrets they do not want to share. At the same time, do not tempt them by sharing unique ideas you hope to implement in the future.

Have you identified business owners with whom you can share ideas?
Yes   No

Outside Experts

An early financial investment in good advice is appropriate when evaluating a new opportunity. Most likely, the first money you spend should be for consultation with professionals trained to give tax, accounting and legal advice. There are many free resources available, as well.

A) Tax and Accounting Advice

A Certified Public Accountant (CPA) can help you understand the ever-changing tax ramifications of self-employment. For instance:

- Employers pay half of the Social Security and Medicare taxes, and the employee pays the other half. When self-employed, you pick up the entire cost for yourself, which currently is 15.3% of personal income.

- Tax rules vary according to the legal form chosen for the business (i.e., sole proprietorship, LLC, S-Corporation, etc.). Tax implications need to be understood before the legal structure is finalized.

- Tax filing requirements. For instance, many small businesses are required to pay quarterly estimated taxes.

- The tax status of benefits paid to owners or employees can vary.

- There are tax consequences of having a home office, particularly if you own your home. Thoroughly check them out in advance.

- State and local tax laws can have unexpected ramifications.

- Retirement planning (e.g., IRA, SEP,401-K).

- Employee issues (e.g., Social Security and Medicare taxes, inclusion of benefits in income calculations, retirement plans, and unemployment insurance).

Another critical issue is to find an efficient way to <u>track ongoing expenses</u>. Business expenses are best monitored if they are segregated from your personal finances. Storing all of your business receipts in a box is a start.

However, it does not have to be time consuming or costly to record expenses in a simple spreadsheet. As the business grows, you can employ a bookkeeping software package, or more formal arrangements can be made if necessary.

Once you select the type of legal entity, you will know which <u>government-issued ID number</u> is appropriate. If you choose to create a sole proprietorship, your Social Security Number (SSN) will be used for identification purposes on bank accounts and IRS-related materials. Otherwise, the business will need an FEIN (i.e., Federal Employer Identification Number, also known as a TIN or EIN), which is the business equivalent of a SSN. A FEIN is available via www. irs.gov.

Use a FEIN or your Social Security Number to establish a dedicated business bank account. If you have multiple credit cards in your household, choose one to use for business expenses only.

<u>Simple, consistent financial organization</u> will help identify the status of expenditures and make tax time easier and cheaper. If necessary, there are on-line bookkeeping services to meet your needs as if they were next door.

<u>Employees</u> add a significant level of complexity from an accounting standpoint.

- Fortunately for small business owners, payroll services can handle tax calculations and make direct deposits. All of your payroll needs can be handled at a relatively low cost, and managed on-line. External payroll services are especially helpful during start-up, or during periods of intense expansion.

- Payroll software packages are available if you or a trusted associate can manage them.

- Consistent and reasonable vacation and personal-day policies must be developed, tracked and documented.

- Reporting needs for health insurance coverage continue to evolve.

- Many small businesses use sub-contractors rather than employees, resulting in less paperwork and administrative overhead. More importantly, as one small business owner observed, contractors tend to be more invested in the work process, which – in turn – leads to a positive outcome for all parties. Of course, sub-contractors are not a viable option for every type of business.

Retail businesses need to offer customers the ability to pay via <u>credit card</u>. Credit card companies charge sellers processing fees, which may vary considerably.

Certain non-Retail businesses (e.g., consulting) send <u>invoices</u> to clients as the work progresses, or upon completion. In those cases, timely and accurate invoicing will be critical for business success. It is almost a crime to send out invoices long after the work has been completed.

Clear and concise invoices should include everything needed for the bill to be paid, and all of the information required for the payer's tax records, such as:

- Your company name and address.

- Invoice number and date.

- Name and address of the person billed.

- Brief description of the services rendered or products sold.

- Amount due.

- Due date.

- Payment address or alternate instructions.

In addition, an <u>invoice-tracking process</u> will be needed to:

- Monitor the timing and dollar-value of invoices sent.

- Monitor the timeliness of payment receipt.

- Initially, a simple spreadsheet should suffice.

Spending some money up-front, to ensure you are as up-to-date as possible on regulations, will allow you to concentrate on your areas of expertise. There are many accounting firms willing and able to help you with these critical issues.

Have you consulted with tax and accounting specialists?
Yes   No

Are you prepared to handle personally or monitor closely the detailed financial activities of your business?
Yes   No

If you are not going handle the details yourself, do you have a trusted person to take care of your invoices and expenses?
Yes   No

B)   Legal Advice

Before you commit to starting a business, determine your legal needs and the associated costs to handle them. Include:

- Legal form of business.

- Contract negotiations with clients, landlords, vendors and more.

- Protection of intellectual property.

- Trademark, copyright or patent protection.

- State, county and municipality requirements.

- Health and safety regulations.

- Payment and reporting of sales taxes.

The importance of legal advice corresponds to the potential size of the business idea and the risks involved. Do not count on what a non-qualified person tells you about these important issues. Websites offering inexpensive legal documents should be used with caution. Legal decisions often require more interaction and assistance than a website can deliver.

The cost of a few hours with appropriate legal professionals can save you a tremendous amount of money later, and provide peace of mind.

Have you met with a qualified attorney?
Yes   No

C)   Insurance Advice

Insurance needs should be considered early in the process of starting a business. A qualified insurance agent who represents a number of companies can be a great resource for advice on:

- Health insurance.

- Business property insurance for theft, fire or other loss.

- Business liability insurance, even if you decide to work out of your home.

- Errors & Omissions (E&O) insurance.

- Life insurance on you, to protect the business and your dependents.

- Disability insurance.

- Unemployment insurance for employees.

Insurance agents do not charge the policy holder for their services. Their income is included in the cost of the policy.

Health insurance can be both costly and time-consuming. The legal and administrative requirements continue to fluctuate. One of my business partners spent many, many hours researching insurance options and making what he believed to be an informed decision. Within a week he was notified of substantial complications, which led to even more hours of research.

Health insurance could be one of the most significant costs to pin down before making a final decision on whether to proceed with a new business. Some companies specialize in health insurance planning for businesses, but finding one willing to work with a startup can be difficult. Be sure to consider the cost of coverage along with the resources required to administer a plan.

All of these insurance costs should be factored into the Financial Plan, which is a critical section in the Business Plan, covered in Chapter 4.

Have you investigated possible insurance products for your business?
Yes   Some No

D) Government Agencies

There are a number of resources offered to prospective entrepreneurs by local, state and federal governments. In addition, understanding the requirements of regulatory agencies may be critical to your success. Do not overlook potentially relevant government input, such as:

- Tax credits for businesses operating in economically disadvantaged areas.

- Local, state or federal guidance at little or no cost. For instance, if your start-up is a child care center, assistance is available in some communities. Such guidance can be instructive when putting together a Timeline, which is covered in Chapter 4.

- Professional licensing and regulations (e.g., for barbers, tradesmen, teachers, psychologists, and health care professionals).

- Health requirements and safety inspections (e.g., for restaurants).

- Home-based business requirements, if any.

Be sure you understand all government requirements and opportunities – as well as any related costs.

Have you researched the possibility of government resources?
Yes   No

Will anyone at your business need a professional license?
Yes   No

Will you be subject to regular government inspections or regulations?
Yes   No

E)   Creative Services

For a start-up, having a consistent "look" over time, including colors, logo and typeface, can help establish recognition and reinforce your competitive positioning. A tag line, describing what the business does, can be instructive for the target audience. Many businesses, both small and large, have them.

For instance, The Entrepreneur's Friend®, my personal business, has the tag line, "Our Work. Our Lives." Together, the name and tag line help describe the entity.

You will need outside assistance if you are not comfortable handling creative work yourself. Generally, most small businesses do not need to hire an advertising agency. There are many free-lance artists, copywriters and editors available to complete relatively small jobs.

When considering an external resource, be sure to review examples of their work and speak with current clients before proceeding. In addition, determine if there are potential conflicts of interest, such as a competitor of yours who is a client of theirs.

Sometimes, we are fortunate enough to have a business partner or family member who can work on various creative options for us. Of course, it is important for them to have skin thick enough to hear "no" or "we need to change this" as a response, without taking personal offense.

Do you know how you would approach creative issues for a start-up?
Yes   Somewhat   No

Do you know how much necessary creative services might cost?
Yes   No

F)   Local Community Colleges

Courses in business, entrepreneurship, communication and more are available for a reasonable price at local community colleges. The instructors will often extend themselves to assist serious students.

If your skills are weak in a particular area (e.g., marketing or accounting), take a course to speed up your learning curve. If you take courses before you begin working full-time on your business, you will be better able to determine which tasks you can handle yourself, and which ones you need to pay someone else to do.

Have you checked the availability of relevant courses in your area?
Yes No

G)   Private Grants

Private institutions offer grants for specific types of businesses, sometimes based on location in narrowly-defined geographic areas (e.g., Detroit). Private grants are available for non-profit operations, as well.

Have you investigated the possibility of a private grant to help with the development of your business idea?
Yes   No

Chapter 4

Deciding Factors:
Estimate Financial Viability

"The plans of the diligent surely lead to profit;
and everyone who is hasty surely rushes to poverty."

Proverbs 21:5 (WEB)

"A picture is worth a thousand words."

Unknown

～ ～ ～ ～

Simply put, an entrepreneur risks an investment of time and resources believing the resulting business will be successful. A viable business generates enough sales to more than cover all of its expenses, even though that breakeven milestone may not happen for months or even years. Out of any resulting profit, the business owner must decide how much to pay him or herself, and how much to invest back into the business to ensure sustained future growth.

Why is a Business Plan Helpful?

The best way to measure financial potential is to construct a Business Plan. Do not let the idea of developing a Business Plan intimidate you – it is the foundation of successful entrepreneurship.

A local classic car restoration expert started his business with an established reputation, rain-makers to refer customers, a waiting list of car enthusiasts anxious to become customers, sufficient insurance, and a professionally-equipped garage in his back yard for him to work on clients' cars. All he needed was a very simple plan.

Few start-ups are so fortunate. Many face significant challenges, such as leases, the need to hire employees and make capital investments. At the same time, most of us need to actively hunt for potential customers and turn them into buyers.

A Business Plan organizes the development process. Every owner should have a written plan, even if it is no longer than a few sheets of paper. In fact, there have been initial business plans written on the back of a napkin. Of course, if your plan is hand-written, make sure you have an extra copy in case it gets wet – or is lost.

A good planning document serves as a road map, enabling you to identify and think through critical issues. Your ability to focus on the most important issues of the business will improve, so you are less likely to become side-tracked by trivia.

Ultimately, Business Plans provide a framework to address every essential aspect as thoroughly as possible, while organizing and prioritizing them, including:

- Product/service design and development.

- Production process.

- Marketing techniques.

- Pricing.

- Product mix, sourcing and distribution.

- Future growth.

- Personnel.

- Analyzing results.

- Legal & accounting considerations.

- Ownership & investment.

- Facilities.

- Accessibility.

- Sales & expense estimates.

- Cash flow.

- Update schedule.

Thorough planning will help minimize unpleasant surprises which could lead to failure. By including a Financial Plan covering three to five years, you will be able to estimate what will happen if you follow a particular road map, and easily update your plan as you learn more.

My last corporate job ended because of downsizing. In a desperate, but ultimately unsuccessful, attempt to save the company, a large portion of the management team was let go. The corporation offered each of us a transitional office and career counseling. However, I knew I wanted to become an independent business consultant.

Therefore, I asked the head of Human Resources to let me "cash out" of the transition services, giving me an equivalent amount of cash to buy equipment and furniture for my new business. He asked me to produce a Business Plan before he would agree. Having previously worked at a consulting firm, I was quickly able to develop a reasonable plan. Even though he did not understand the consulting world, the plan persuaded him I could be successful, and he authorized my "cash out."

Do not spend money on a potential business without a Business Plan, with the possible exception of conferring with an attorney and/or a CPA (i.e., Certified Public Accountant). Too many people have boxes in their attics or garages filled with products or supplies they purchased too soon and will never use.

Even worse, some people have expensive leases for facilities where their business needs cannot be met. Plan first. Then, spend.

One of the tremendous advantages of self-employment is you can set your own goals and deadlines. But, you need to remember them, and refer to them often. The documentation provided by a Business Plan enables you to build your own structure based on reasonable assumptions. As you proceed, your Business Plan should serve as a yardstick for you to measure and evaluate your progress.

As a result of the planning effort, you will have a solid assessment of the business's potential to share with a bank, financial investor(s), possible business partner(s), or other outside entity, if needed. A thoughtful plan demonstrates your dedication to the new venture, even if changes are suggested, requested, or required by other interested parties.

Elements of a Business Plan

Start with a plan for the first year. If potential seems likely, then extend it. Many new businesses do not become profitable for several years, particularly if they require a high level of up-front investment. That is why the basic outline for a strategic Business Plan should span three to five years.

A Business Plan always starts with the big ideas. As we move through the plan, each section becomes more specific. Development is an iterative process, with each section likely to impact others. Therefore, consistency and coordination between sections are required.

There are eight primary elements of a Business Plan. Details on these key sections follow, including:

- Business Objectives (i.e., WHY will this business exist?).

- Mission Statement, based on the Business Objectives.

- Strategies (i.e., in broad terms, WHAT will be done in order to achieve the Business Objectives?).

- Tactics (i.e., specifically, HOW will the Strategies be supported?).

- Strengths & Weaknesses.

- Next Steps.

- Timeline.

- Financial Plan.

Special note: [x] designates a place where your specifics would be inserted.

Section I: Business Objectives

WHY will this business exist? What are the big goals?

We all set objectives for our business, whether we recognize it or not. These are probably what drove us to consider self-employment in the first place:

- I don't want to move.

- My brother-in-law wants me to work with him.

- I need to make enough money to send our kids to college.

- This looks like something I could do.

- My body hurts too much to keep doing my current job.

These are all legitimate personal objectives. They may help define what the business is, but they do not define what the business will do. On their own, they will not make you successful.

Business Objectives are different. Starting a business requires specific business goals. If you do not have a target, there is no way you will ever hit it. Large packaged goods companies start by defining Objectives, but you do not have to be big to employ the same planning process.

Objectives are not about how you will do something, but what it is you want to do over the longer term. These are the big goals. Everything you invest in your business should help you achieve these Objectives in some way.

There can and should be multiple Objectives, but having too many can cause you to lose focus. Three should be plenty, but some companies include as many as four or five.

Try using one of each of these types of Business Objectives, in your order of priority:

- Income targets. Start with your best guess – whether pie-in-the-sky or conservative. Income for you or revenue for the company, whichever is most appropriate.

- Focus on a particular field, industry, or product/service.

- Character of the business.

For example, Business Objectives might be:

- Build a plumbing business to: 1) generate a reasonable income for me and any employees, 2) build a loyal base of repeat customers, and 3) reflect my personal values of respect and responsibility.

- Become a published author who can: 1) bring pleasure/knowledge to the lives of others, 2) generate $[x] income to cover future family education costs, and 3) share my spiritual beliefs.

- Build a medical practice to: 1) provide quality medical care in the field of pediatrics, 2) generate $[x] income for the physicians and other employees, and 3) devote [x] % of practice appointments to low-income patients.

- Create a consulting practice to: 1) aid businesses in the [x] industry by providing [x] services to grow sales and improve efficiency, 2) generate $[x] in annual income for owner(s) within five years, and 3) provide a work environment resulting in strong employee loyalty.

If you have business partners, it is critical you all agree in writing on your mutual objectives. Agreement on the relative priority of each objective is particularly important.

For instance, is the primary goal to generate cash distributions now or to build the business by investing a great deal of the profits in equipment and employees? Confusion or conflict concerning key objectives can cause major disruption among the partners.

If you proceed with your start-up, frequently review your list of written objectives. Documented objectives can be powerful, keeping you focused on your goals.

Have you identified clear Business Objectives?
Yes   No

Section II: Mission Statement

A Mission Statement is a succinct sentence or two describing your entity. It is the equivalent of an "elevator speech" – your concise answer to "tell me about your business" in the length of time it takes to ride an elevator five floors. Once Objectives have been identified, it is easier to sum them up into a single statement.

The Mission Statement for my business, The Entrepreneur's Friend®, has helped me measure the appropriateness of various opportunities: "Offer practical guidance, encourage character development, and share spiritual insight to help others plan, start and grow businesses."

It is worth taking time – right now – to clarify your thinking by writing down key words and ideas to describe your vision.

Can you describe your business idea in a concise Mission Statement?
Yes   No

Section III: Strategies

A Strategy is a broad look at <u>WHAT</u> ideas, concepts or changes are needed to help us meet our Objectives. For example, one Strategy for a new child care center could be to understand the local competition in order to offer a superior situation to parents. Another might be to serve parents by providing care outside of the schedule offered by the competition.

Strategies should address every area necessary to achieve your Objectives. For example, here are a few basic Strategies, suitable for many businesses:

Objective: Generate $[x] of Gross Income annually within five years

Strategy: Develop a viable Financial Plan demonstrating the possibility of achieving financial goals.

Strategy: Develop marketing procedures to introduce the product line to potential customers and encourage repurchase from existing customers.

Strategy: Develop new products and/or expand product lines to increase sales by at least [x]% per year.

Strategy: Acquire a physical location within budget, suitable for the needs of the business, well located and physically secure.

Objective: Focus on [specific] Industry

Strategy: Work in [specific] industry based on [experience, knowledge, opportunity, etc.].

Strategy: Position (i.e., describe) the business as offering high quality at a fair price.

Strategy: Closely monitor competition for possible opportunities and threats.

Objective: Create a healthy work environment

Strategy: Develop highly motivated and engaged personnel.

Strategy: Contribute to the welfare of the local community.

Strive to list at least one or two Strategies for every Objective. If you cannot come up with any, the Objective may need to be re-considered. Some Strategies may be appropriate for more than one Objective.

Strategies are – by design – somewhat vague, allowing you look at the big picture (i.e., the important steps you should be taking) rather than becoming engrossed in the details (i.e., how you are going to accomplish this).

Have you thought through the essential ideas (i.e., Strategies) necessary in order to reach your Objectives?
Yes   No

Section IV: Tactics

Tactics flesh out <u>HOW</u> the Strategies will be implemented. Tactics are the specific tasks that need to be completed in order to execute one or more Strategies. Building on the earlier child care strategy example, the following tactics would make sense: To understand child care competition you must talk to 1) parents of children currently in child care, 2) parents who are looking for child care and 3) child care workers and preschool teachers. To serve parents by broadening the care hours, tactics could be to offer 1) overnight and/or 2) weekend care.

Tactics are derived from, and are supportive of, your Objectives and Strategies. They are the defined, measurable and achievable actions necessary to turn a Strategy into reality, enabling you to achieve your Objectives. They are the point at which planning begins to look like action.

Obviously, Tactics should be relevant and feasible. Aim for at least one or two Tactics for every Strategy, but list as many as you believe would be helpful. You do not need to implement them all immediately. By thinking them through and documenting them in the plan, you are more likely to achieve your goals. In addition, they will provide the specific input necessary for developing a Financial Plan. (See Section VIII.)

With the addition of Tactics, the plan becomes more firmly defined. By way of example, here are potential Tactics for some of the Strategies and Objectives shown previously:

Objective: Generate $[x] of Gross Income annually within five years

Strategy: Develop marketing procedures to introduce the product line to potential customers and encourage repurchase from existing customers.

- Tactic: Develop a name that is memorable, does not cause confusion, and is available to trademark.

- Tactic: Hire a design team to create a logo, tag line, and consistent "look" in advertising, including type face and color selection.

- Tactic: Develop appropriate "touch points" (i.e., points of direct customer contact, such as a website, phone call, direct mail, trade show, etc.)

Strategy: Develop new products and/or expand product lines to increase sales by at least [x] % per year.

- <u>Tactic</u>: Monitor the sales of each existing product.

- <u>Tactic</u>: Develop unique accessories for key products.

- <u>Tactic</u>: Seek available, appropriate products and product extensions (e.g., lampshades, extension cords and surge protectors, if you currently offer lamps) from outside suppliers.

<u>Strategy</u>: Acquire a physical location within budget, suitable for the needs of the business, well located and physically secure.

- <u>Tactic</u>: Total cost, including utilities, should not exceed $[x] per month.

- <u>Tactic</u>: Include at least [x] square feet, with the possibility of expanding into nearby space.

- <u>Tactic</u>: Office should be within 30 minutes of a regional airport to minimize time for traveling employees and visiting clients.

- <u>Tactic</u>: Conference space will be necessary for regular meetings.

- <u>Tactic</u>: Dedicated work space for each employee.

- <u>Tactic</u>: Parking area should be well lighted after dark.

- <u>Tactic</u>: Limited access to the location outside of business hours.

Objective: Focus on [specific] Industry

<u>Strategy</u>: Position the business as offering high quality at a fair price.

- <u>Tactic</u>: Develop high quality products.

- <u>Tactic</u>: Set pricing after studying the competition and determining the cost of product creation.

- <u>Tactic</u>: On an ongoing basis, find ways to maintain or increase quality while decreasing costs.

- <u>Tactic</u>: Ensure safety in order to minimize down-time and resulting inefficiencies.

- <u>Tactic</u>: Incorporate strong quality control measures to eliminate the distribution of flawed product.

- <u>Tactic</u>: Develop strong relationships with reliable suppliers/vendors, viewing them as members of the team.

Objective: Create a healthy work environment

<u>Strategy</u>: Develop highly motivated and engaged personnel.

- <u>Tactic</u>: On the first day of employment, set clear expectations.

- <u>Tactic</u>: Hire independent contractors who can become full-time employees as conditions warrant.

- <u>Tactic</u>: Train employees in customer relationship skills (e.g., removing shoes when doing repair work in the home, leaving a business card).

- <u>Tactic</u>: Give two Personal Days annually, allowing employees to attend family events, such as sporting events for their children, award ceremonies, etc.

- <u>Tactic</u>: Give employees one day off each year to work at a Habitat For Humanity build.

<u>Strategy</u>: Contribute to the welfare of the local community.

- <u>Tactic</u>: Sponsor a youth soccer team.

- <u>Tactic</u>: Donate up to [x] products/services to local fund-raisers.

- <u>Tactic</u>: Give employees one day off each year to work at a Habitat For Humanity build. (Note: A Tactic may support more than one Strategy.)

Tactics may be large or small, long-term or short-term, but they will all translate into the foundation of your "to-do" list.

Most importantly, do not become entangled in trying to perfect the elements of your Business Plan. For instance, sometimes a Tactic can also be a Strategy.

Overall, the planning process can be an extraordinarily helpful tool and provide a disciplined way of thinking. Use it in the way that best serves your needs.

Have you identified the specific tasks (i.e., Tactics) you need to accomplish?
Yes   No

Section V: Strengths & Weaknesses

Here, the honest evaluations you have done about yourself, and the research you have conducted with outside sources, will pay off. In addition, the process of formulating Objectives, Strategies and Tactics should have made Strengths and Weaknesses easier to identify.

List the evaluations of your necessary skills, talents, employee pool, financing, competitive advantages, and more. Be honest, so you will know what needs to be addressed in order to reach your goals.

For example, if you are not comfortable with numbers, that should be identified. Or, you might be a superstar with spreadsheets, but need help communicating with prospects and customers. By identifying all of these, you will acknowledge improvement is not only necessary but possible.

Sometimes it is difficult to see our own abilities and limitations because we take them for granted – or, we are in denial that they exist. If you have partners, include them in the development of a company-wide list. Focus on the importance of working together to strengthen the business. You will need to create an open, trusting environment by sharing some of your personal weaknesses. Otherwise, the process can turn into destructive finger-pointing.

Brainstorm with others to develop an extensive list of Strengths & Weaknesses. Think broadly about the business, both in the near and longer term. Will there be additional opportunities once the business is operational? What potential threats should be monitored?

Here are a few assets that may be important to your business. Do you have them now (i.e., Strengths) or are they missing (i.e., Weaknesses)?

- [x] years of experience in a similar business.

- Hours of operation.

- Bilingual.

- Strong financial footing.

- Available credit line for cash flow.

- Unique products, trademarks, patents, etc.

- Qualified team members for necessary positions.

- Cost-effective production.

- Smooth, timely payroll system.

- Broad product line for future sales.

- Parking.

- Industry contacts who will refer business (i.e., rainmakers).

- Marketing experience.

- And more.

Of course, no one is perfect. The best advice my husband ever gave our now-grown children has been: "Build on your strengths and learn how to compensate for your weaknesses."

What do you need to improve about yourself or your business in order to maximize the potential for success?

Have you identified at least five weaknesses in your business?
Yes   No

If not, try again.

Have you identified at least five strengths?
Yes   No

If you have more weaknesses than strengths, identify more strengths, or consider whether it is advisable to continue down the path of entrepreneurship without making significant adjustments.

Section VI: Next Steps

What will you need to do first? And, what comes next? The Next Steps section of the Business Plan includes specific actions based on everything you have documented so far.

Break each Tactic down into well-defined tasks with deadlines. For instance:

Tactic: Develop strong relationships with reliable suppliers/ vendors, viewing them as members of the team.

Next Steps:

- Create a list of potential suppliers.

- Research potential fit with your business.

- Select top contenders.

- Tour the facilities.

- Check references.

- Negotiate an agreement that is fair to both parties.

- Meet with key contacts on a regular basis.

- Invite key contacts to participate in annual planning meetings.

Tie the resulting "to-do" list to the Business Plan with a due date assigned for each task. Include start dates, particularly for tasks taking place over a long period of time.

Adjust the level of detail to what is required for your circumstances. Seek a balance between over-complicating the process and making sure nothing is overlooked. Some of these tasks will involve other people or companies. Their due dates will impact your timeline, and vice-versa.

When setting dates, be realistic. At the same time, challenge yourself. Do not make the dates so aggressive you become frustrated, or so spread out you do not move forward in a timely manner. After all, you are the boss. The dates can always be adjusted if necessary.

Do you have an initial list of tasks to do, both short-term and long-term?
Yes   No

Section VII: Timeline

A Timeline has two purposes in our Business Plan.

First, identify the order in which all Next Steps should happen.

Once you have made a list of Next Steps with a deadline for each, it is a relatively simple matter to put all of the dates into chronological order. Determine the best order in which the tasks should be accomplished.

Look for periods of time on the resulting schedule in which there is too much or too little to do. Adjust those now, during the planning stage. If you wait, it can become impossible to adjust later, or you may have to make tough choices that could have been avoided. Additional changes will be necessary as your plans evolve.

Second, identify the Critical Path.

Highlight the tasks that absolutely have to happen, and are contingent upon the completion of other tasks on the list. Collectively, these are known as the Critical Path, or the essential tasks that must be completed for progress to occur.

The following items are likely to be on the Critical Path for a start-up. Note they are numbered to show order. However, some have the same number, indicating both must be completed before moving on to the next task. Be sure to add a due date for each.

#1 – Determine a company name.
#1 – Settle on the type of legal entity (e.g., sole proprietorship, LLC or S-Corp).

#2 – Apply for a Federal Employment Identity Number (FEIN), unless you are going to be a sole proprietor and use your Social Security Number.

#3 – Open a bank account, using the name and FEIN (or SSN). Deposit working capital into the account to cover initial expenses.
#3 – Apply for a credit card dedicated to your business, unless you are going to dedicate an existing personal credit card for business only.

#4 – Begin making purchases using capital you have set aside for the start-up, either by way of checks, cash or credit card linked to your business bank account.

When identifying your Critical Path, first consider the tasks requiring interactions with outside entities, especially legal, financial, zoning and licensing. These can be big stumbling blocks if they are not handled in a timely manner – and some of what you find out may be surprising.

For example, a friend was going to start a child care center in her home. She had a viable concept, built on a solid business plan. She went to great lengths to borrow money for a 7-passenger van, as specified by government regulations.

Unfortunately, she did not realize she had to get her landlord's approval before the center could open in her rented home. As of now, she has a van and is looking for a new, more appropriate home. In the meantime, she is not bringing in income to help pay her car loan.

When new equipment, new human processes or new software is integral to your success, allow time for testing, re-testing, and testing again until successful. Lack of proper testing has caused the delay of many start-ups. Caution generally dictates a phased rollout over time, if possible. Allow problems to be resolved as the business builds, prior to a full market introduction.

Have you developed a realistic Timeline and identified the Critical Path?
Yes   No

Section VIII: Financial Plan

Financial Plans are essential to your Business Plan. They allow you to deal with uncertainty in an orderly way. You will want to come up with reasonable assumptions to reflect your best possible understanding of the next three to five years, based on the Objectives, Strategies and Tactics you have identified. Prospective bankers and investors appreciate the professionalism of a well-thought-out Financial Plan.

The most telling part of the plan is when you apply dollars to the Tactics you have developed. You should be able to determine if a profit can be generated – and when. Early in the process, many of the assumptions will be estimates, or even guesstimates. However, you will still gain important perspective.

Developing a Financial Plan will reveal if something is out of alignment: sales, costs, or timing. By laying it all out in logical fashion, changes can be made now to improve the situation – immediately, as well as in the long run.

A married couple decided to start a business after doing their homework on a specific service industry. By doing a detailed financial plan, they concluded the best business approach would require much more capital investment than they were willing to commit. As a result, they brought in a former co-worker as a partner, sharing the financial risk. Eight years later, all parties have been happy with the outcome.

Business owners go through all of the effort, and take the sometimes-significant risks, in order to generate income for themselves and others. If your plans do not point to profitability within a reasonable period of time, then you need to re-think them. If your plans indicate marginal results, you may want to walk away because, generally speaking, costs are always higher and progress slower than initially estimated.

The Financial Plan should be organized into a simple Profit and Loss Statement (i.e., P&L):

- Gross Revenue, also known as Gross Sales. (100% of the money received for goods & services)

- Subtract Adjustments, such as:
  - Returns, credits, and refunds.
  - Sales taxes collected.

- Equals Net Revenue, also known as Net Sales.

- Subtract Cost of Goods or product-related expenses, such as:
  - Raw materials to create products for sale.
  - Associated processing costs.

- Equals Gross Profit, also known as Gross Margin.

- Subtract Operating Expenses, such as:
  - Personnel (e.g., employees and independent con-

tractors).
- Sales and Marketing (e.g., advertising).
- Overhead (e.g., space, insurance, equipment, and utilities).

- Equals <u>Income from Operations</u>.

- Subtract <u>Other Expenses</u>, which are based on Income from Operations:
  - Profit distributions to you and any partners.
  - Taxes.

- Equals <u>Net Profit</u>. Often referred to as "the bottom line."

Guidelines for Financial Assumptions

- The Financial Plan should be developed in an electronic spreadsheet. There are very good, sometimes free, templates available on-line to calculate your bottom line based on your specific input. Other techniques (e.g., hand-written and hand-calculated) are not as flexible or easy to change, even though any well-considered plan is helpful regardless of methodology.

- Separate the fixed costs (i.e., those that do not vary based on the volume of products or services produced) from the variable costs (i.e., costs that do change based on the number you buy or produce).

- Organize the plan into twelve monthly columns, with a total for the year. Do not worry about tying to a calendar year until later.

- Subsequently, expanding the plan to three to five years will help you understand the long-term implications of your beginning assumptions.

- Initially, look at the timing of cash outlays and cash revenue, without considering the tax accounting and long-term investment implications. The resulting Cash Flow plan is a critical element for banking and investment considerations. Tax considerations can be can be added later, with the help of an accountant.

- Allow for some "wiggle room" in your assumptions, so some number of negative changes will not put the business at risk. In every start-up, circumstances change. Delays occur. Estimates will be incorrect. People will let you down. Therefore, do not assume every aspect will work smoothly.

- Start simply and expand the spreadsheet as you develop additional details. For example:
  - How many products or "service units" (e.g., consulting hours) do you think you can sell?
  - When? How many a week or month?
  - How much will you charge?
  - Will you be collecting sales tax(es)?
  - How will customers pay (i.e., cash, credit card or check)? Note: credit cards can incur significant fees.
  - When will income be received? The payment methods offered will directly impact the timing of income. If you send invoices, keep in mind some payments will be late.
  - What are the expenses, both fixed and variable?
  - When will expenses need to be paid?
  - If you bill by the hour, how will your weekly hours be split between billable (i.e., paid by a client) and non-billable (e.g., buying office supplies, talking to prospective clients, and handling payroll)? How quickly will the number of billable hours increase? The ratio of billable to

non-billable hours can be one of the most difficult to predict. It is very easy to overestimate billable hours, and underestimate non-billable hours.
  ○ Will there be "economies of scale"? In other
    words, as the number of items produced for sale
    goes up, will the cost per item produced go down
    because of increased efficiency?

The most important result of developing a Financial Plan
is clarification of possible Net Profit (i.e., the profit remain-
ing after subtracting expenses from income) or Loss. Once
you have some bottom-line insight, take time to reflect:

• What are your criteria for success or failure?

• Will planned income cover the expenditures required?
  If you have to spend more in a month than you take in,
  how will you supply the difference?
  ○ Slow payments will impact your credit rating and
    your future ability to borrow.
  ○ Cash flow is particularly critical if you will have
    an employee payroll, or significant sums are
    owed to creditors. Employees do not want to
    work if they are not sure they will be paid.

• Are there realistic limitations?
  ○ Example #1: If you want to have a hair salon, but
    you would have to work eighty hours a week to
    cover standard local rent and utilities, you could
    not possible generate much in the way of per-
    sonal income. Would you be better off sharing
    a somewhat bigger space with another stylist, or
    working fewer hours? Or, should you/can you
    work out of your home?
  ○ Example #2: What if ten thousand units a year
    must be produced to cover costs (i.e., breakev-

en), but there are only a few hundred people in the target audience – and, they each might buy only one or two units? Ever. In that case, you need to rethink your entire business plan.

- What should be adjusted?
  - o In an electronic spreadsheet, it is fairly simple to generate various scenarios in the search for the best planning alternative.
  - o Sales generally occur more slowly than expected. Use caution in your timing assumptions by planning for a slow start. Then, work to improve when the business opens.
  - o Once you have the first set of results for your Financial Plan, assume different growth in future sales and/or changes in costs, and see how the results change.
  - o If product costs will decrease dramatically as quantities increase, use "rollout" or "full production" costs as part of your evaluation. Basing your plan on the higher initial costs during a test or start-up phase may lead you to make a poor long-term decision. However, actual start-up costs must be considered in any cash-flow scenario.
  - o Add more detail if doing so will clarify your thinking.
  - o Tie any changes back to specific Strategies and Tactics, identifying what you need to do to make these changes happen.

If your "picture" of the future is not viable, change your assumptions and try again. You will want to settle on a viable plan with higher than expected costs – because costs are almost always greater than anticipated.

An important benefit of the financial detail is <u>investment requirements</u> will be more clearly defined. Since there can be significant benefits and risks related to every option, in-depth study should be given to possible funding sources, including:

- Personal savings. Be sure to keep enough for living expenses and any other critical needs.

- Home equity loan. Use extreme caution here, as your personal home would be tied to the new business, potentially risking both.

- Bank loan. Some collateral will be needed by the bank, possibly your home.

- New partners. Management participation will need to be clearly defined along with the amount of financial investment.

- Outside investors. Management participation may be required, as well.

Keep in mind any investor will push hard to minimize the risk of losing his or her investment. The same should be true for the entrepreneur who is starting the business.

One of the values of a Financial Plan is it forces us, if we are honest with ourselves, to face our costs and the timing for each in advance. As a result, we end up with a cash flow plan to aid us in interactions we have with our bank or other financial institutions, and plans for any significant expenditures or investments. Once we commit to start a business, the Financial Plan becomes a critical yardstick for measuring success.

Have you developed an initial Financial Plan?
Yes   No

Does your Financial Plan demonstrate a reasonable chance for viability?
Yes   Maybe   No

Have you identified necessary changes?
Yes   No

Evaluating Your Business Plan

For some, the end result of a Business Plan will be the realization that the business, as currently structured, is not viable. If so, the plan will have served its purpose. We always benefit from discovering insurmountable problems before significant investments have been made.

On the other hand, your Business Plan may confirm your concept is a good one. The process of developing a plan may have increased your confidence and streamlined the start-up process.

Or, you may find the idea worthy of consideration, but choose to pursue education, gain relevant experience, or solidify your personal finances before proceeding.

By thinking through all of the elements in a Business Plan, you will save yourself time, energy and headaches in the months and years ahead. By avoiding recognizable problems in the beginning, you will be better prepared for the challenges ahead.

Have you developed a written Business Plan?
Yes   No

Does it include the basic elements listed?
Yes   No

Have one or more copies of your written plan been saved on-line (i.e., in "the cloud"), at a second physical location, or in a safety deposit box?
Yes   No

Chapter 5

Deciding Factors:
Realistic Expectations

"To make no mistakes is not in the power of man;
but from their errors and mistakes the wise and good learn wisdom for the future."

Plutarch

"The best thing about the future is that it comes one day at a time."

Abraham Lincoln

≈ ≈ ≈ ≈ ≈

Choose Reality, Not Fantasy

Remember those election speeches in elementary school? Some of the candidates for school office would promise whatever they thought it would take to get a vote, such as more recess or free ice cream every day. Promises that could not be fulfilled. Those who gave their vote to someone making unrealistic promises definitely chose to live in a fantasy world.

Too often we tell ourselves half-truths – or avoid thinking about difficult issues – rather than facing facts. Truth always wins out in the end, and any delay in confronting it may make the resulting pain worse.

For example, there are multiple costs associated with adding employees. Everyone expects the monetary cost. However, there are also non-monetary costs, such as the emotional investment associated with the process of hiring, training, and mentoring. A good manager takes seriously the responsibility of helping provide a roof, food, health care and educational expenses for the families of their employees. The reality of hiring human beings requires us to take business ownership very seriously. Their problems can become our problems.

As a mental health professional once told me, "Living in the real world, rather than one built on fantasy, is the best indicator of good mental health." Be intellectually honest with yourself. Do not blindly tell yourself everything will turn out great unless you have done your business homework through good planning, or if you have generated some proven success.

Be honest not only with yourself but with others. Trustworthiness is one of the most rewarding character traits you can ever demonstrate – for you and your business.

Are you prepared to be realistic about the requirements of business ownership?
Yes Maybe No

Common Causes of Business Failure

All-too-frequent reasons for new business failure must be recognized so they can be avoided. Be prepared. Take these common causes of failure into account as you proceed:

- Poor business planning:
  - No contingency planning for unexpected growth or too-slow sales.
  - Weak inventory management.

- o Too heavily invested in fixed assets.
- o Ineffective employee scheduling.
- o Failure to evaluate past performance.
- o Poor location.
- o No evolution or growth planned.
- o No Plan B in case of failure.
- o Production inefficiencies.
- o Dependence on a single customer.

- Marketing deficiencies:
  - o Inability to attract first-time buyers.
  - o Unable to generate repeat sales from previous buyers.
  - o Blindness to competitive challenges.
  - o No on-line presence.
  - o Weak Customer Service.
  - o Inadequate Public Relations in a crisis.
  - o Inappropriate pricing.

- Poor financial management:
  - o Inadequate cash to get through slow sales periods.
  - o Excessive cash distributed to owners.

- Management problems:
  - o Disagreements with partners than cannot be resolved.
  - o Lack of personal commitment.
  - o Burnout.
  - o Lack of leadership.
  - o Dissatisfied employees.
  - o Lack of a succession plan.

- Unexpected considerations:
  - o Declining demand for products or services.
  - o Family health issues.

○ Theft of intellectual property.
○ Loss of property not covered by insurance.
○ Cultural differences.

Have you built safeguards into your Business Plan in order to minimize the negative impact of these common problems?
Yes   Somewhat   No

The Goal of Sound Business Planning is to Establish Realistic Expectations

Is there a good chance for success? What key issues could cause disaster if they were to change?

Sometimes the reason for disaster is completely unexpected. A married couple was anxious for the husband to leave a job in the corporate world requiring extensive travel. As book lovers, they first considered an independent book store. But, industry changes made that option less attractive. Then, they settled on a bakery.

Well-versed in business and marketing, the couple invested a significant amount of their savings in their new venture. They catered continental breakfasts for local businesses, in addition to their consumer sales. They did everything right – except see the on-coming low-carbohydrate health trend. As bread sales tanked, they lost their entire investment.

A young dentist, fresh out of dental school, worked arduously on rehabilitating an old home in the historic section of his city. The plan was to have his practice on the first floor and live upstairs.

The problem? He did not understand how long it takes to build a dental practice when most patients only come once or twice a year. After a year with an almost empty schedule, he joined the staff at a local hospital. He discovered income was more important than office charm.

Disaster is not inevitable, but you need to pay attention. One man developed a business based on deep expertise in commercial product sales. Great sales people are incredibly optimistic. Unfortunately, he was not experienced in managing the less exciting details of a business. His unwillingness to face facts, or get someone to help him do so, took him into bankruptcy.

Another couple floundered at entrepreneurship because neither of them liked to balance the check book. They were afraid of what the balance might tell them about their situation. Not an auspicious approach to financial success.

There will always be surprises and road-blocks along the way because that is the way life unfolds. Life is not fair. However, speed bumps are less likely to surprise you when you have identified them, and have a plan to manage them. Road blocks seen from a distance can help you turn to new, successful paths.

Once an honest financial plan has been developed, you will be in a position to make an informed decision about whether to pursue the new business. Do your homework until you are ready to proceed with your business opportunity, decide to put it on hold pending further study, or choose to walk away. Include your spouse, along with trusted members of your personal community, in your thinking process. These steps will complete your start-up sanity check.

If you choose to start a business, be realistic but optimistic. Small business ownership can be a fulfilling and satisfying adventure for those who are prepared.

Are you being realistic in your thinking?
Yes   No

Is it clear to you how you should proceed?
Yes   No

Are you ready to start your own business?
Yes   No   Wait

"Beloved, I pray that you may prosper in all things and be healthy, even as your soul prospers."

                                        3 John 1:2 (WEB)

About the Author

Cynthia Baughan Wheaton has life-long ties to entrepreneurship, and has been educated by new business successes as well as failures. Cynthia earned a BA in English at Meredith College, along with studies in Business Administration. She also obtained an MBA from The University of North Carolina at Chapel Hill at a time when few women sought one.

As a manager, Cynthia developed new ventures within L'eggs Direct, then a division of Hanes Corporation, and at World Book Encyclopedia. At Kestnbaum & Company, she learned the consulting business. After a decade as an independent database marketing consultant, she joined forces with her husband to create Wheaton Group LLC, a successful boutique consulting firm.

Cynthia's website, www.TheEntrepreneursFriend.com, offers encouragement, practical advice and spiritual insight in hundreds of articles for self-employed people. In addition, her current social media accounts are identified, so you can follow the latest perspectives on an entrepreneurial life.

Made in the USA
Columbia, SC
12 January 2021

30849073R00050